THE CHERNOBYL DISASTER

Essential Events

THE CHERNOBYL DISASTER

BY MARCIA AMIDON LUSTED

Content Consultant
Sarah D. Phillips, PhD
associate professor of anthropology
Indiana University

ABDO
Publishing Company

CREDITS

Published by ABDO Publishing Company, 8000 West 78th Street, Edina, Minnesota 55439. Copyright © 2011 by Abdo Consulting Group, Inc. International copyrights reserved in all countries. No part of this book may be reproduced in any form without written permission from the publisher. The Essential Library™ is a trademark and logo of ABDO Publishing Company.

Printed in the United States of America,
North Mankato, Minnesota
112010
012011

 THIS BOOK CONTAINS AT LEAST 10% RECYCLED MATERIALS.

Editor: Mari Kesselring
Copy Editor: David Johnstone
Interior Design and Production: Marie Tupy
Cover Design: Marie Tupy

Library of Congress Cataloging-in-Publication Data
Lusted, Marcia Amidon.
  The Chernobyl Disaster / by Marcia Amidon Lusted.
     p. cm. -- (Essential events)
  Includes bibliographical references and index.
  ISBN 978-1-61714-763-0
  1. Chernobyl Nuclear Accident, Chornobyl', Ukraine,
1986--Juvenile literature. 2. Nuclear power plants--Accidents-
-Ukraine--Chornobyl'--Juvenile literature. 3. Chornobyl'
(Ukraine)--History--20th century--Juvenile literature. I. Title.
  TK1362.U38L87 2011
  363.17'99094777--dc22

                           2010045019

TABLE OF CONTENTS

*In 2010, a commemoration ceremony in Kiev, Ukraine,
marked the twenty-fourth anniversary of the Chernobyl disaster.*

1:23 A.M.,
APRIL 26, 1986

*I*t should have been a simple safety test to
see how long the nuclear plant's turbines
would run if they suddenly lost electric power. The
Chernobyl nuclear power plant, in the Ukraine
region of what was then the Union of Soviet Socialist

Republics (USSR), already had three operating reactors to produce electricity. Reactor Number Four had been commissioned, but one vital test had never been performed. Under pressure from the Soviet government to complete the reactor and make it operational, Viktor Bryukhanov, the man responsible for the construction and operation of the Chernobyl plant, had not tested the turbines and how long they would continue to make power if they were to lose electricity. In the event of a power loss, the electricity produced by the still-spinning turbines would be enough to fill the gap before emergency generators would start up, to power the reactor's cooling systems. The test was considered vital enough to be required before any reactor went online, but in this case it had been overlooked.

In late April 1986, two years after Reactor Number Four was officially commissioned, the Soviet government in Moscow learned that this test had not yet been conducted and sent a representative to oversee

The Advantages of Nuclear Power

Nuclear power is a popular energy source because the fissioning of one atom of uranium produces 50 million times more energy than burning one atom of carbon (found in fossil fuels such as coal and oil). The energy generated by three small pencil eraser–sized pellets of nuclear fuel is equal to that of 3.5 short tons (3.2 t) of coal or 12 barrels of oil. With uranium more plentiful and cheaper than oil or coal, it is an attractive form of energy.

it. They decided to conduct the test in the early-morning hours of April 26, when demand for electricity would be low, since the reactor would not be able to provide power during the testing. Bryukhanov himself was not even present at the time. He entrusted one of his engineers, Anatoly Dyatlov, to supervise the testing. Shortly after midnight, they began the procedures to lower the amount of energy the reactor generated.

A Series of Mistakes

The procedure was supposed to be simple. First, the reactor's output would be reduced to a level where the turbines could be disconnected from the reactor. Then, engineers could measure how long the turbines continued to spin without power. However, a series of poor decisions would haunt this simple test. The emergency alert system was temporarily shut off so that it would not read the test as a real accident. But this also disabled the pumps that could send water to cool the reactor in case it overheated. In addition, there were far fewer control rods—which were inserted into the reactor to control or stop the nuclear reaction process—than there should have been.

At 1:23 a.m., the test began, but just before the turbines were to be disconnected, the operators in the plant's control room realized that the water level in the reactor had fallen to a dangerously low level. The reactor was overheating, its energy levels rising rapidly. As the temperature increased, the pipes that carried the water to cool the reactor burst from extreme pressure. Immediately afterward, another explosion shook the building. The lights flickered out. Powdery dust filled the air. In just a few seconds, radioactive dust and debris ripped the roof off the building surrounding Reactor Number Four and shot into the night sky. Large chunks of the reactor's graphite core were thrown out of the hole and then rained down on the surrounding area, starting more fires. Air rushed into the destroyed reactor building and ignited what was left of the graphite core into a volcano-like glowing mass.

A Dubious Track Record

Before the Chernobyl disaster, the USSR already had a history of minor nuclear accidents. There was an accidental explosion and radiation leak at a Leningrad (now known as St. Petersburg) power plant in 1974. A power plant in Beloyarsk had a near meltdown in 1978. A meltdown occurs when the uranium in the reactor overheats and melts, releasing radioactive material.

Most Soviet power plant workers firmly believed that these plants were safe, even though they were following safety guidelines that were developed in the 1960s for much smaller reactors. And because the USSR did not release news of these accidents to the country or the world, most people never knew they were in danger.

Years later, Dyatlov would write a letter to a friend, describing how he felt at that moment:

It seemed as if the world was coming to an end . . . I could not believe my eyes. I saw the reactor ruined by the explosion. I was the first man in the world to see this. As a nuclear engineer, I realized all the consequences of what had happened. It was a nuclear hell.[1]

Sasha Yuvchenko, an engineer and mechanic in the control room that night, was getting supplies from a storeroom down the hall when the explosions occurred. "There was a heavy thud," he remembered, "A couple of seconds later, I felt a wave come through the room. The thick concrete walls were bent like rubber."[2] The two explosions completely destroyed Reactor Number Four, but that was just the beginning. The accident at Chernobyl would be—and remains—the worst-ever release of radioactivity from a nuclear power plant.

Soviet Union Politics

Employees of the Chernobyl plant did not understand what the radiation could do to them. The firefighters who were immediately called to the scene did not wear any protective clothing, nor did plant employees. The Soviet Union had always maintained that having a disaster plan in place would make the public feel that an accident was possible. Since the government publicly insisted that the nuclear plants were completely safe, no one questioned the lack of emergency plans at the plant. This absence of foresight would ultimately result in hundreds of deaths, both immediately following the Chernobyl disaster and in the months and years to follow.

The Soviet Union also insisted on withholding any news from the public that might give it a negative image. Any kind of

How Does It Work?

How does a nuclear power plant generate electricity? At a nuclear power plant, a nuclear reaction produces energy. The energy heats up a system of circulating water to create steam. The steam is then used to spin the blades of a turbine, and the turbine creates electricity. But how does the reactor produce this energy? It starts with a fuel called uranium, which is one of the largest elements in the periodic table. Uranium is called an unstable element because its atom is too big to stay together permanently. When a uranium atom is bombarded with a neutron in a process called induced fission, it splits and produces a huge amount of energy.

Once the fission process begins, it sets off a chain reaction with the other atoms, creating more and more energy. However, to keep this chain reaction from getting out of control, a nuclear reactor also has a series of control rods, which can absorb the neutrons that create fission. Like their name suggests, they control the fission process. They can accelerate fission when they are withdrawn from the reactor and act like a brake when they are inserted. If the nuclear reaction needs to be halted quickly, the operator of the nuclear plant can drop all the rods into the reactor, where they absorb all the neutrons and halt the reaction. This is called scramming.

Why Is Nuclear Power Dangerous?

The dangers of using nuclear energy come from the products that result from the fission process. During fission, in addition to energy, a certain amount of radio-activity is also released. It is extremely poison-ous to humans, animals, and plants. Large doses of radioactivity interfere with cell growth and can result in cancer, and even death.

There are four types of radiation. Each moves through the human body in a different way. Alpha rays cause skin redness and can lead to heart problems years after expo-sure. Beta rays can reach internal organs through the skin and cause cells to mutate or become dam-aged. Gamma rays are very dangerous. They can affect the thyroid gland, internal organs, and bone marrow, usually causing cancer. Neutrons are the most penetrating type of radiation. Human expo-sure to neutron radiation can lead to cancer.

accident or disaster might make other countries think that the USSR was weak or that its system of government did not work. As a result, the public did not hear the truth about the Chernobyl accident and the possible health effects until it was often too late to protect themselves.

The accident at Chernobyl was the result of a combination of poor decision making on the part of those who built and operated the reactors, and a basic reactor design that was flawed. Accidents of all types can and do happen anywhere in the world, often despite the best planning. However, the decisions the Soviet Union would make about the disaster at Chernobyl would have a devastating effect on both its own people and others around the world.

Chernobyl's Reactor Number Four was completely destroyed during its testing procedure.

Moscow, the capital of the Soviet Union, was a bustling city in the 1980s.

IN THE BEGINNING

I n the 1980s, the Soviet Union was a country in desperate need of more energy. At that time, it had more land area than any other nation in the world, more than 8.6 million square miles (13.8 million square km). It also had a population of approximately 270 million people. A country with so much land and so many people had an insatiable appetite for electricity. Following World War II and the development of nuclear power, first as a weapon and then as an energy source, the Soviet Union became one of the world's leading nations in the use of nuclear power to generate electricity.

More Power!

Despite the number of reactors it had in operation, the USSR needed still more energy. It already had a power plant in the Ukraine, which was a republic of the Soviet Union, located southwest of the city of Moscow. At the time, the Ukraine was an agricultural region, producing grain and other crops that were used to feed the entire country. Its capital city was Kiev (spelled Kyiv in Ukrainian), and the city was supplied with water from a huge reservoir created by a dam on the Dnieper River. On the shores of this reservoir was a small, old village called Chernobyl. Fifteen miles (24 km) farther north was the modern city of Pripyat. Pripyat had a population of approximately 49,000 people. On a flat area between Pripyat and the village of Chernobyl, the V. I. Lenin Power Station opened in 1977. Most

*Volodymyr Shashenko, a Chernobyl engineer,
and his family lived in the town of Pripyat in the Ukraine.*

people simply called it the Chernobyl nuclear plant.
It had three nuclear reactors and generated enough
electricity for the millions of people living in Kiev,
Pripyat, and even most of the western portion of the
Soviet Union. Pripyat itself had been constructed
in the 1970s expressly to house the nuclear plant
workers and their families.

But the three reactors operating at Chernobyl still were not enough to meet all the power needs of such a huge nation. The Chernobyl reactors were a type known as RBMK. Because the USSR needed so much electricity, Soviet engineers had increased the size of these RBMK reactors beyond their initial design. The core of each reactor was a huge mass of graphite, weighing more than 2,500 short tons (2,268 t), which was used to control the nuclear fission process. This graphite core was drilled with more than 1,000 holes. Some of the holes were for the fuel rods filled with uranium. Some were for the insertion of the control rods, which could regulate the nuclear reaction and shut down the reactor if necessary. RBMK reactors also did not have the protective containment structures that nuclear plants in other parts of the world, such as the United States, have.

Five Year Plan

The Soviet economy was organized around a government-approved system called the Five Year Plan. These five-year plans set out a series of often unrealistic goals or objectives that were supposed to be accomplished within that time period. Those who failed to meet their five-year plan goals were usually demoted or sent on other assignments in remote locations.

It was decreed that the first four reactors of the Chernobyl plant were to be built according to a five-year plan. This set a dangerous precedent. Trying to follow a schedule that was created by men hundreds of miles away in the government, who had no real knowledge of nuclear power and its dangers, seemed foolhardy. However, the engineer in charge of construction, Viktor Bryukhanov, had no choice but to meet the plan, even if it meant that corners were cut and construction was sometimes shoddy. Bryukhanov also had trouble getting the highly specialized parts he needed to construct the reactors. So, some of the parts, such as valves, piping, and pumps, were actually built on the grounds of the plant itself. However, these parts were not the ones that the nuclear designers had specifically approved for use in their reactors.

Bryukhanov's Management

Bryukhanov's methods for meeting the five-year plan on the construction of Chernobyl were admired, both by those who worked for him and by the Communist Party officials who governed the country and created the plans. Bryukhanov's management of the nuclear construction led to the commissioning of Reactor Number Four three months ahead of schedule. Bryukhanov received a bonus for his work. Soviet leaders could now boast that the plant was generating not only enough electricity for the western portion of the Soviet Union, but enough to supply parts of eastern European countries such as Poland.

But there was no opportunity for Bryukhanov to enjoy his accomplishments. A new five-year plan called for the construction of two more reactors, and the foundations were already being poured for Reactors Five and

Build a Town, Too

Viktor Bryukhanov did not just have the responsibility for constructing the Chernobyl nuclear plant. He was also in charge of ensuring there would be enough workers to staff the plant. The best way to do this was to attract them with a modern and attractive city. Pripyat was a city planned with the power plant in mind. Bryukhanov wanted to attract the specialists and workers needed at Chernobyl, so he created Pripyat with shopping centers, museums, good schools, athletic facilities, and even an amusement park. He hoped these amenities would entice young Soviet workers to come and stay. The city was located in an area with beautiful forests, streams, and lakes for hiking, fishing, and recreation.

Pripyat soon had a population of more than 45,000 people. The average age of its residents was 26. Young couples and their children loved the new city, and it was only one mile (1.6 km) from the huge Chernobyl power plant.

Zhores Medvedev wrote about the governmental policies that caused the rushed construction of the Chernobyl reactor.

Six at Chernobyl. Soon, the Chernobyl plant would be the largest nuclear power plant in the world. In addition to the responsibility for constructing more reactors, Bryukhanov was also addressing problems with the first three reactors. In 1985, after a scientific study, the Ministry of Energy and Electrification in Moscow ordered Bryukhanov to replace the roofs on the turbine buildings so that they would be fireproof. Bryukhanov now had the difficult task of finding enough fireproof material to cover such huge expanses. Safety inspectors had also found that many of the cables used in the reactor buildings did not have a fireproof covering. When Bryukhanov explained he had been unable to obtain this material, he was allowed to leave them the way they were. It was common in Soviet industrial construction for government commissions to approve a project as complete, even when there was still a long list of elements or operations not yet completed. According to Zhores Medvedev, a scientist who was forced into exile from the USSR, in his book *The Legacy of Chernobyl*:

> If the commission takes a straight line and refuses to sign an act of acceptance, no one receives a bonus and basic salaries may be delayed. Everyone, including the government, is unhappy if the plan is

Bitumen

When Bryukhanov was ordered to replace the roofs of the buildings in the Chernobyl plant, it was because they were originally constructed using a material called bitumen. Bitumen was used for waterproofing and as an ingredient in asphalt for roads. It was also highly flammable. Bryukhanov had argued that he could not purchase enough fireproof material to re-cover the roofs, which were slightly under one mile (1.6 km) long and 164 feet (50 m) wide. The roofs were still covered with bitumen at the time of the explosion. The raining chunks of graphite quickly ignited small fires everywhere on them. The burning bitumen also created clouds of thick, black smoke. Firefighters attempting to put out the fires said it was like walking on tar.

registered as unfulfilled. The result is that it has become normal practice to accept as fully operational industrial objects that have not been completed to specification.[1]

A Fateful Decision

Under pressure from the Soviet leadership to construct and operate these reactors, Bryukhanov was forced to depend on his supervising engineers, such as Anatoly Dyatlov. So, when Bryukhanov was ordered to perform the turbine test, he decided to entrust Dyatlov to supervise the test. Bryukhanov was scheduled to be in Kiev at that time, where he was meeting with Communist Party leaders about plans for the new reactors. So, even though Dyatlov had never supervised a safety test before, Bryukhanov left him in charge. It would be the first of several fateful decisions that led to the Chernobyl disaster.

Viktor Bryukhanov

Viktor Bryukhanov was director of the Chernobyl V. I. Lenin power plant from the beginning of its construction in 1970 until the Chernobyl disaster. He was 50 years old at the time of the accident. He became a delegate to the Communist Party Congress in 1985, representing the Kiev region. Until the accident, party leaders and those who worked for Bryukhanov admired his management of the construction and operation of the Chernobyl plant.

Workers at the Chernobyl plant in 1980

*Workers inspected fuel channels above the core
of Chernobyl's Reactor Number Three.*

CHERNOBYL'S REACTORS

*I*t was the third Sunday in December 1983,
a day that is traditionally a celebration
day for workers in the energy industries of the
USSR. Most professional groups in the USSR had
their own day of celebration every year, which was a

chance for the press to publicize what they did and an opportunity to present awards and pay bonuses. So, what better day could there be to announce the completion of yet another brand-new nuclear reactor in Chernobyl's power plant?

Because a nuclear reactor is such a complex piece of machinery, it usually takes six months from the time when the reactor is actually operational to when it is ready to produce power on a regular commercial basis. But because Reactor Number Four at Chernobyl had received so much attention in December, Bryukhanov was under pressure from the Soviet government to get the reactor operating at full power on a regular basis much sooner than the usual six months. It would be a victory for the government, especially since other nuclear reactors had been delayed in becoming operational.

A Complex Machine . . . with a Flaw

The nuclear reactors that the Soviet Union built were of several different types, but the type at Chernobyl was the RBMK reactor. In Russian, RBMK is an acronym for *reaktor bolshoy moshchnosty kanalny*, which means a "reactor of large power with channels." These reactors, built only in the USSR, were less expensive to build because they did not require enriched uranium. They could also produce plutonium for use in nuclear weapons. Like other types of reactors, the RBMK used boiling water to create steam, which, in turn, powered turbines to produce electricity. It also used graphite (the same substance found in pencils) to control the nuclear fission process. There was also an emergency cooling system that would inject cold water into the reactor core and shut the reactor down if the fission process went out of control.

The RBMK reactor, however, had several design flaws. It was vulnerable because the many pipes and welded joints that were used to provide water in the event of an emergency were subject to leaks or faults. If the supply of electricity to the reactor itself was interrupted, the emergency cooling system would not work until emergency generators started up. The reactor was also designed to allow the fuel rods to be changed without actually shutting down the reactor. This meant that there needed to be large cranes above the core to extract the rods, so the reactor itself was approximately 230 feet (70 m) tall.

The reactor's height made it difficult and expensive to construct an emergency containment structure for it. Emergency containment structures were concrete domes, such as those used on nuclear reactors in Western countries. If the pressure inside the reactor were to rise high enough, the top could blow off the reactor structure. Without a containment structure, there was no extra layer of protection between the reactor and the outside atmosphere. Additionally, since the same water that moved through the core and boiled to produce steam was then cooled again and recirculated to cool the reactor, a break in the piping system could reduce the amount of cooling in the reactor.

Even before the accident in Reactor Number Four at Chernobyl, power plants in other parts of the Soviet Union that used RBMK reactors had already discovered design problems that had never been addressed. If these reactors were run for a long period of time on less

Keeping It Cheap

Why were the Soviet RBMK reactors built without containment domes unlike those in the United States and Europe? It was all about economics. A concrete containment dome big enough to cover a tall RBMK reactor would be extremely expensive to build. The USSR was focused on the construction and operation of the reactor itself. Safety concerns were secondary, and indeed, the government felt that adding expensive safety features and emergency plans would make the public less trusting of nuclear energy.

than half power, they became unstable. As a result, the reactor core could overheat. The usual reaction to an overheating reactor core is to drop all the control rods into the core to stop fission, which was known as scramming. In regular water-cooled reactors, scramming only took about four seconds, but in a RBMK reactor, it could take as long as 18 to 20 seconds to insert all the control rods. When a nuclear core is overheating, every second counts. Those extra seconds would allow the core to continue

China Syndrome

One of the biggest fears with the use of nuclear power is the so-called China syndrome. It gets its name from the hypothesis that if a nuclear reactor were to go out of control and become too hot, it could melt through the crust to the core of the Earth itself and all the way through to China. As early as the 1960s, scientists on the Advisory Committee on Reactor Safeguards were already considering this possibility. As a result, they asked the nuclear industry in the United States and Europe to come up with safeguards that would prevent this scenario from ever occurring.

However, the China syndrome gained even more publicity after a 1979 movie of the same name. The plot was loosely based on incidents that took place at the Rancho Seco Nuclear Power Plant in California, but in the movie, and at the California plant, the power plant shut down exactly as it was designed to do in the event of an accident.

In March 1979, an accident took place at the Three Mile Island Nuclear Power Plant in Pennsylvania, which eerily mirrored the events of *The China Syndrome*. The reactor overheated, and a small amount of radioactivity was released into the atmosphere. However, the reactor was cooled before a meltdown could occur. While the incident led to new safety protocols in nuclear plants in the United States, it also heightened public fears over nuclear plant safety.

overheating, which would boil the water in the cooling system, turning it to steam and ultimately resulting in an explosion.

The USSR's engineers, rather than redesigning the entire system, decided the simplest solution to the RBMK's problem of overheating on low power was simply to run these reactors at high power all the time. This meant all the components of the reactor, such as piping, joints, and moving parts, were subject to a great deal of wear.

In September 1982, an event occurred that warned of the RBMK's dangers. When Reactor Number Three at Chernobyl was in need of maintenance, due to this kind of wear, reducing the power gradually resulted in the overheating of several fuel assemblies and a minor explosion before the control rods could be inserted. Although this released a small amount of radioactivity into the air, the emergency cooling system worked and cooled the reactor. Yet, this incident did not serve as a warning to the engineers at the Chernobyl plant. Instead, the Communist Party leaders were angry that Reactor Number Three was out of commission for several months for repairs, which would cost the government money.

TESTING, TESTING . . .

Party leaders were congratulating Bryukhanov for building Chernobyl's fourth reactor and having it ready for operation months ahead of schedule. In the rush to announce to the country that yet another marvel of Soviet technology was ready to produce power, it was quietly ignored that many of the tests required before a nuclear reactor could begin operating commercially had been overlooked. Since the process usually required six months, the only way to shorten that was to reduce the number of tests, either postponing them or simply not doing them.

Chernobyl Reactor Number Four had been officially accepted for commercial operation. Those involved received their bonuses, awards, and other extra rewards for finishing the plant ahead of schedule. Overlooking the fact that many crucial tests had not yet been performed or had not given satisfactory results, everyone was pleased. It was a victory for the USSR and its nuclear power program. But Bryukhanov and his team had no way of knowing just how devastating this "victory" would become.

The RBMK reactors of Chernobyl had several design flaws.

The control room for Reactor Number Four in 2000

IT WAS JUST A TEST...

With the start-up of the Reactor Number Four, scientists and academics all over the USSR were full of praise. Academic Aleksandr Yefimovich explained, "We were delighted to hear of a remarkable achievement."[1] When asked about whether the public would be alarmed at the continued construction of so many nuclear plants, Yefimovich said, "People can be very emotional about these things. The nuclear power stations in our country are perfectly safe for the populations of the surrounding areas."[2] His words would soon come back to haunt him.

A Fateful Test

The plant was officially commissioned, but all those tests that had been postponed or not completed satisfactorily still had to be run, in particular, testing the turbogenerators. It was essential to know just how long the turbogenerators—which spun and generated electrical energy from the steam produced by the nuclear reactor—would continue to spin, even after electrical power failed at the rest of the plant.

The turbogenerators were a very important part of the reactor's safety system. The plant's emergency generators could not start up immediately if power failed. These diesel-powered generators took three minutes to start, much longer than the backup generators in Western nuclear plants, which only took ten seconds to reach full power. It was essential to have emergency power as quickly as possible, since electricity was necessary to run the pumps that sent cooling water to the reactor, and also to lower the control rods into the reactor and stop the fission process. If these systems lost power, the reactor could quickly overheat and cause a meltdown of the reactor's nuclear core. It was essential to know how long the turbogenerators would continue to spin after a loss of power, and how long they could continue to operate the cooling system and the control rods.

The test was scheduled for shortly after midnight on April 26, 1986. With Bryukhanov out of town, Dyatlov was in charge. Reporting to him were Aleksandr Akimov, a foreman, and his men. Nuclear engineer Leonid Toptunov and plant engineer Sasha Yuvchenko were also there to observe the test.

The power in the reactor had to be reduced gradually. One of the by-products of nuclear fission is the gas xenon, which can absorb neutrons without splitting. If the fission process were reduced too quickly, the excess xenon gas would absorb neutrons so quickly that the entire fission process would shut down. This could cause an explosion. If the power reduction were to take place gradually, the xenon gas could decay without shutting down the entire fission process.

As the power declined to 50 percent over a 12-hour period, one of the two turbines powered by Reactor Number Four was shut down, since two turbines could not run off half power. Power in the reactor would then be reduced to 30 percent, at which point the second turbine could be switched off, and the engineers could time how long the blades continued to spin. If the blades did not spin for the required 45 to 50 seconds, which would allow time for the emergency diesel generators to start, then the technicians could repower the turbine and repeat the test.

It was 2:00 p.m. on the afternoon of April 25, and the first turbine had been disconnected from the reactor. The technicians were getting ready to reduce power and disconnect the second turbine when

"It was like airplane pilots experimenting with the engines in flight!"[3]
—*Soviet scientist Valery Legasov, on what took place during the turbine test*

Dyatlov—who had never supervised this kind of test before—realized that shutting off both turbines would decrease water flow between the turbines and reactor. If the test could not be performed within the specified amount of time, the backup generators would start, triggering the emergency alert system and flooding the reactor. Dyatlov gave the order to disconnect the emergency alert system temporarily. However, just as the test was about to begin, Dyatlov received a call from the Ministry of Energy in Kiev. More power was needed in the region, so the test would have to be postponed. Instead of returning the reactor to full power, it was left running at a little below 50 percent for the rest of the day, a situation in which the RBMK reactor was known to become unstable.

Another Try

At midnight, it was time to resume the test. With the emergency system shut down, Akimov and Toptunov's only information from the reactor was a computer printout across the room from the control panel. They would have to balance the number of control rods inserted in the reactor with the amount of neutrons being absorbed by the xenon gas.

Without the emergency alarm system, they would not know whether power levels dropped too low in the reactor. At 12:30 a.m. on April 26, the printout told the technicians that the reactor level had fallen to less than 5 percent power. The test should have been abandoned, and the reactor shut down completely, but Dyatlov was eager to get the test over with. Instead, he ordered that seven of the 18 control rods in the core be removed to increase fission and raise power for the test.

Because the reactor had been operating at low power for more than 12 hours, the water-cooling process was not working as quickly as it should have. However, with no emergency alert

Confusing Instructions

Scientist Valery Legasov was a member of the commission sent to Chernobyl shortly after the accident. In an article published after his death, he maintains that the operators in the control room that night did not understand what the test was about:

I have in my safe a transcript of the operators' telephone conversations on the eve of the accident. Reading the transcript makes one's flesh creep. One operator rings another and asks: "What shall I do? In the programme there are instructions of what to do, and then a lot of things are crossed out." His interlocutor thought for a while and then replied: "Follow the crossed out instructions."[4]

However, Legasov did not place all of the blame on the operators. He maintained that many people had been involved in the creation of the confusing instructions and the lack of training provided to the plant's workers.

Two explosions destroyed Reactor Number Four.

system operating, there was no way to know this in the control room.

At 1:23 a.m., Dyatlov told the technicians to go ahead with the turbine test. As they started, Toptunov noticed that the power in the reactor was now rising too quickly, heating up too fast. Akimov told Dyatlov that he was going to activate the emergency switch and lower all the control rods into the core at once, to stop the nuclear fission.

THE CATASTROPHE

When Akimov lowered all the control rods into the core at once, it caused a power surge. The reactor produced 100 times its normal amount of power in just four seconds. As the temperature rose in the reactor, the fuel channels ruptured, and water was able to flow into the reactor space. However, this created a sort of nuclear volcano, as the water instantly became steam and exploded. Only 20 seconds after the activation of the emergency switch at 1:24 a.m., the first explosion damaged the roof of the reactor building, lifting an upper steel and concrete plate that weighed more than 1,000 short tons (907 t). The second explosion was caused by hydrogen and shot chunks of red-hot graphite from the reactor into the sky.

Because a RBMK reactor does not have a containment building, and because the graphite modulator was still in the reactor, the nuclear fission process was actually continuing. The water that worked as a coolant was lost, but the chain reaction of nuclear fission continued, with nothing to moderate it. So, while the reactor building was destroyed, and chunks of graphite and debris were raining down around the Chernobyl plant, the men in the control room and those who would arrive to help did not yet realize that the greatest danger was one that they could not see—radiation.

Who Is at Fault?

When asked for his opinion about whether the operators were responsible for the procedures that led to the accident, operator Igor Kazachkov said, "There should not just be highly qualified people at the control panels, but freer people. Free from fear. People who aren't afraid of the sword constantly hanging over their heads. You know . . . what does it mean to be fired from work at Pripyat? That's it, the end. . . . If [Aleksandr] Akimov had been free, then he would have been able to make the correct decisions."[5]

A satellite image taken a few days after the explosion
shows the Chernobyl plant in blue and its adjacent cooling pond.

Long after the Chernobyl accident, dosimeter readings at the site are still 30 times above normal radiation levels.

FIRES, CONFUSION, AND CHAOS

*I*n the moments following the first explosions at Chernobyl's Reactor Number Four, Yuvchenko grabbed a flashlight and, with three other men, made his way down the hallway that led to the reactor building. On his way, he met a worker whose face was bloody and covered with blisters. The man could barely speak, only point down the hallway to the reactor building and whisper that three men were trapped in there.

Yuvchenko stayed outside the reactor hall, holding the door open with his shoulder while the other three men went inside. Those three men all died within two weeks because of the massive amounts of radiation they were exposed to inside the reactor building. Yuvchenko, who survived, later said:

> You don't feel anything at the time. . . . We had no idea there was so much radiation. We met a guy with a [device for measuring the amount of radiation an individual is exposed to] and the needle was just off the dial. But even then, we were still only thinking, "Rats, this means the end of our careers in the nuclear industry."[1]

A man named Valery Khodemchuk had been on duty in the reactor, just above the concrete plate that covered the top, when the explosion occurred. He was the only immediate victim of the explosion. A second reactor operator, Vladimir Shishenok, who had been close by was still alive when he was found, only to die about an hour later.

The reactor building was open to the sky, and flaming lumps of graphite from the reactor core had been blown out of the building and onto the surrounding roofs and grounds. Altogether, there were approximately 30 fires in different parts of the Chernobyl plant, in addition to the graphite fire in the reactor crater itself. The first thing that needed to be done was to put out the fires.

Rushing In

The fire alarm sounded at the local fire station in Pripyat only minutes after the second explosion. Three fire engines and their crews were the first to arrive on the scene at the plant at 1:28 a.m. Their commander, Lieutenant Vladimir Pravik, quickly realized that the scope of the fires was beyond what his small crew could confront. He sent a coded radio message calling for more firefighters from stations in Pripyat, the town of Chernobyl, and the whole surrounding region of Kiev.

From the outside, it was easy to see the extent of the damage. Half of the roof of Reactor Building Number Four was gone. There was a hole in the side of the building that looked directly into the core, which was lit by an eerie glow. The firefighters immediately entered the reactor hall. More crews arrived and entered other sections of the reactor building to fight the fires there. Fires were also burning on the roof of Reactor Building Number Three, and that reactor was still operating. This put Reactor Number Three in danger of exploding as well. The firefighters knew they had to extinguish these fires quickly, but they were hampered by the bitumen roofing material. The bitumen had caught fire from the falling debris and was difficult to extinguish. The firefighters positioned themselves on the remains of the Reactor Number Four roof, aiming their hoses at Reactor Building Number Three.

The firefighters managed to extinguish all the fires except for the burning graphite core. However, most of them did not realize that they had been exposed to a deadly amount of radiation from the core. They did not have the specialized clothing or equipment necessary to fight a fire in a nuclear plant.

Amazingly enough, Reactor Number Three continued to

Protecting Firefighters

Firefighters who are trained to fight fires in nuclear power plants have specialized equipment, such as protective suits and self-contained breathing apparatuses. This equipment protects their bodies from radiation exposure and prevents them from having to breathe air that could be contaminated with radiation. The firefighters who first responded to the Chernobyl fires had no special equipment at all.

operate despite the accident, although the night-shift supervisor wanted to shut it down. There had been a severe increase in radioactivity as radiation penetrated the third reactor through the ventilation system. Finally, at 5:00 a.m., it was shut down. By that time, the fires were out, and the immediate danger of flames spreading to the entire plant was over.

NOTIFYING THE GOVERNMENT

Bryukhanov returned to Chernobyl from Kiev at 2:30 a.m. He had been awakened by a phone call from the plant, saying only that some sort of accident had occurred in the fourth reactor and that it was bad. As he made his way to the plant and the control room, Bryukhanov could see the extensive damage to the exterior of the reactor building. In the control room, he talked to Dyatlov and Akimov, but all they could tell him was that the reactor had been in working order right before the explosions. Both men were in shock and also beginning to suffer from the effects of radiation, such as dizziness and nausea.

At 3:00 a.m. Bryukhanov called the nuclear power director in the Communist Party Central Committee, Vladimir Vasilyevich Marin, to report what he knew of the incident. By then, the civil defense chief of the plant, S. S. Vorobyov had arrived and took a reading of the radioactivity present. Radioactivity is measured in units called rems. A reading of 3.6 rems would be considered high. When Vorobyov measured the number of rems in the air, the needle of his machine went off the dial at more than 250 rems. At first, Bryukhanov thought there was something wrong with the instrument, but it was true. A reading this high meant that everyone in the plant and on the grounds had received doses of radiation that could

What Is Rem?

When radioactivity was first discovered in the early twentieth century, the amount of radioactivity given off by substances such as uranium was measured in roentgens, the measurement of radiation exposure. They got their name from Wilhelm Roentgen, the scientist who discovered X-rays, which are radioactive rays that are similar to gamma rays. Eventually, scientists learned just how harmful the different types of radioactivity could be to the human body, and they developed more specific forms of measurement.

The units used to measure the amount of radioactivity at the time of the Chernobyl accident were rems. *Rem* stands for "roentgen equivalent man" and is a unit that measures the actual dose of radiation that a human body absorbs. Adult workers in a nuclear power plant are supposed to receive no more than 5 rems per year, but the body will not start to show effects of radiation until it has received at least 25 rems in a short period of time.

For comparison, the average US citizen receives a dose of .62 rem every year just from natural background radiation, medical procedures such as X-rays, and the natural radiation found in food.

A Bird's-Eye View

On Sunday, April 27, government officials took a helicopter ride above the scene of the accident. They reported what they discovered, "It was evident from the first flight that the reactor was completely destroyed. The top cover which . . . seals the reactor compartment was almost vertical . . . the top part of the reactor hall was completely destroyed. . . . From the nature of the destruction it was clear . . . that an extensive explosion had taken place. A white column several hundred meters high consisting of the products of the fire (apparently graphite) was constantly being emitted from the reactor crater. Inside the reactor space one could see separate huge spots of crimson incandescence."[2]

be deadly. The firefighters and the employees of the Chernobyl plant who were there at the time of the accident would soon show symptoms of radiation poisoning.

However, under the law of the USSR, all accidents of any kind, including nuclear accidents, were to be kept as state secrets. As the people of Pripyat and the surrounding areas awoke on the morning of April 26, they had almost no way to know that just going about their normal activities could be dangerous or even fatal. ⌐

When seen from a helicopter, the damage
from Reactor Number Four's explosion was apparent.

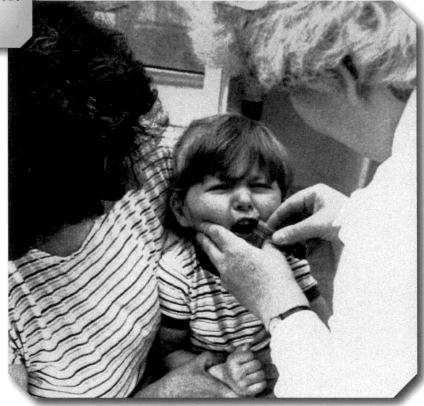

*Nurses gave an iodine solution to patients
to combat radiation poisoning.*

THE FIRST EFFECTS

wo hundred men had fought the flames at
Chernobyl's Reactor Number Four, and
in just these few short hours, many of them had
received fatal doses of radiation. Shift workers in the
plant itself were also feeling the effects of radiation

poisoning. They were dizzy and nauseated; some started vomiting. Others complained of a funny taste in their mouths, which seemed like a combination of chocolate and metal. Most of the firefighters were already becoming weak and had to be evacuated to the nearby hospital. Plant workers wore personal dosimeters. These devices had already hit their maximum reading.

The Chernobyl plant itself had a medical area, staffed with a duty nurse or health officer, but it was closed at the time of the accident. Pripyat's medical service was open, but with only a small staff. The doctor on duty, Valentin Belokon, made his way to the nuclear plant along with two ambulances. He was the first doctor on the scene. Years later, he described the situation:

> *Three people came to the ambulance . . . with headaches and the same symptoms—blocked throat, dryness, nausea, vomiting . . . I was alone and I put them straight into the ambulance and sent them to Pripyat.*[1]

Belokon's ambulance, which he was using as a place to treat patients, was parked close to the damaged reactor. He soon began to feel ill himself, with a sore throat and headache. He eventually became delirious as well and would have to be hospitalized for months in Moscow.

Many workers also suffered from radiation burns, some so severe that the blistered skin was hanging off their arms, caused not from contact with actual flames but from the massive doses of radiation they had received. Others with severe exposure developed thick, rubbery mucus that made breathing difficult, and a rash that formed crusts on their faces and lips.

A Deadly Cloud

While workers and firefighters were being taken to hospitals—many of them dying within the first few hours or days—the nearby city of Pripyat was also beginning to feel some of the effects of the disaster. Because the firefighters used the only method they knew of to fight the core graphite fire, they had poured huge amounts of water into the hole where the graphite was burning. This created a huge cloud of radioactive steam that blew toward Pripyat.

It was a beautiful, warm spring Saturday, and the residents of Pripyat—because of the USSR's policy of not publicizing accidents—did not know that anything serious had taken place at the Chernobyl plant. Even when Soviet troops arrived and circled the plant to keep any observers out, and despite the constant traffic of ambulances and shuttles carrying the injured and sick workers to Pripyat, most people never suspected that anything was wrong. They were outside enjoying the day, sunbathing, fishing, and celebrating special occasions.

Soon, however, people began coughing, vomiting, and tasting that strange metallic chocolate taste in their mouths. One man was sunbathing on the roof of his apartment building and noted that he had never tanned so quickly before. Within hours, he would be taken to the hospital, unable to stop vomiting, and a few weeks later he would die from radiation poisoning. People saw the streets of Pripyat being washed down with

Signs and Symptoms

Just what are the signs of radiation poisoning? The symptoms and their severity depend on how much exposure the person has had, how strong it is, and the distance between the victim and the source of radiation.

The first signs of radiation poisoning are nausea and vomiting. The amount of time that goes by between the radiation exposure and these first symptoms indicates how much radiation the person has absorbed. They will usually appear within hours of exposure. After these first symptoms appear, the victim may have a period of time when there is no apparent illness, but followed by more severe symptoms. Other early symptoms include headache and fever.

More serious symptoms usually follow within weeks. They include dizziness, disorientation, weakness, and fatigue. This is followed by hair loss, vomiting blood, bloody stools, infection, wounds that do not heal, and low blood pressure.

decontaminants. Phones had been cut off as well. But officials still refused to order an evacuation of the town, insisting to the public that radiation levels were normal.

As Saturday, April 26, wore on, word of what had happened in Chernobyl began to filter into the town, particularly as the families of those workers and firefighters who had been rushed to the hospital learned of the injuries and went to see their family members. Lyubov Kovalevskaya, a local journalist whose husband worked in the Chernobyl plant, remembered that morning:

> Nobody said anything. Well, they said there was a fire. But about radiation, that radioactivity was escaping, there was not a word. [My daughter] Anya came back from school and said, "Mama, we had physical exercise outside for almost a whole hour." It was insanity.[2]

It was vital that the residents of Pripyat be evacuated, since the amount of radioactivity in the air was well above safe limits. Officials also knew that radioactivity levels were still rising, but the entire city of Pripyat had been sealed off on Saturday morning, and no one was allowed to leave. Around noon, officials instructed citizens to stay indoors.

Н. В. ВАЩУК

В. И. ИГНАТЕНКО

В. Н. КИБЕНОК

В. П. ПРАВИК

Н. И. ТИТЕНОК

В. И. ТИЩУРА

A Russian newspaper displayed the photographs of six firefighters who battled the fire, and later died from radiation exposure, at the Chernobyl power plant.

Evacuation

Finally, officials began making preparations to evacuate Pripyat. They ordered more than 1,000 buses from Kiev to mobilize. The buses arrived in Pripyat in the middle of the night on Saturday,

Number of Deaths

According to official government reports, 31 people died (mostly firefighters and plant operators) as a result of the explosions at Chernobyl. Twenty-four more people were permanently disabled. One hundred and thirty-four people were diagnosed with acute radiation syndrome from exposure. Twenty-six of these people died within weeks of the accident. Nineteen more died between 1987 and 2004 and their deaths are only suspected to be a result of the accident. No one knows for sure how many subsequent deaths have occurred, and will continue to occur, as a result of radiation exposure in surrounding areas.

April 26. At 2:00 p.m. on April 27, after the residents of Pripyat had already been exposed to radiation from the burning reactor core for almost 36 hours, Soviet military commanders finally gave the order to evacuate the city. Residents were ordered over loudspeakers to pack only one bag to take with them, with enough clothing for three days. But many people in Pripyat already suspected that they would never return to their homes.

Thirty thousand people were loaded into buses, cars, and trains in just a little more than three hours. They were to be taken to what was thought to be a safe zone, 18 miles (30 km) from the plant. But in the following days, as the radiation levels increased, they would be moved farther away still, along with 135,000 residents of other towns, villages, and farms that were located within 18 miles (30 km) of the plant. They would never return home.

When residents departed from Pripyat, they left an entire city vacant.

*In 1986, Chernobyl employees did not have
the proper protective gear such as gas masks.*

GOVERNMENT RESPONSE

he accident at Chernobyl was the largest
nuclear accident ever to take place.
The initial fire had been put out, sending many
firefighters and plant workers to the hospital with
radiation poisoning. But where was the government?

Troops and a Commission

Less than two hours after the accident, according to an article by Colonel General Vladimir Pikalov, commander of the Chemical Service of the Soviet Army, all units of troops in the chemical service were alerted by emergency alarms. The first to arrive at Chernobyl were based in Kiev. They were the first people to arrive at Chernobyl wearing appropriate protective clothing and masks.

Soon, a special government commission had been set up to address the disaster. One of the members of this commission, Valery Legasov, is said to have made many of the key decisions about how to handle the reactor fire. He himself did not even hear about the accident until ten hours after it had taken place. He was told to go immediately to the airport for transportation to the Chernobyl site:

> When we disembarked at Kiev the first thing we saw was a large cavalcade of black government cars and an anxious crowd of Ukrainian leaders. They did not have detailed information, but told us that the situation was bad. We loaded ourselves into the cars quickly and drove to the nuclear station. I must say that it did not even enter my head that we were driving towards an event of global magnitude. [1]

Legasov's account of the events following Chernobyl suggested that officials in Moscow did not yet realize the scope of the catastrophe they were facing.

There were also indications that Moscow was moving slowly in order to maintain the impression that everything was business as usual and that nothing terrible had happened. The Soviet government felt that if there were no outward sign that anything bad had happened, then perhaps no one would take notice of what had occurred at Chernobyl.

As representatives from Moscow arrived at Kiev, they did not expect to be there for more than two or three days. Some of them visited the site of the accident in person and were surprised to see chunks of graphite lying around. When one official asked about measuring the radioactivity levels, he was told that there had been only one radiometer at the plant and that it had been buried somewhere. He replied, "It's outrageous! Why does the station not have the necessary instruments?" A Chernobyl worker replied, "The accident wasn't in the plan. The unthinkable has happened…"[2] It was later discovered that those chunks of graphite were radioactive enough to deliver a lethal dose.

*Radiometers are needed at nuclear power plants
to measure radioactivity levels.*

The chemical troops started to measure the
radioactivity levels around the plant. They found
that those levels were actually increasing through the
night of April 26. It was only later that night that it
was definitely determined the graphite core of the
reactor was burning, releasing enormous amounts of
radioactivity and heat.

On the morning of April 27, after the nuclear
experts and government troops had discussed their
findings at the site, they reported to the commission,
who then reported to the central government in
Moscow. This was the first time the actual scope

Shut Them Down!

After the accident, the entire site of the Chernobyl nuclear plant was heavily contaminated, but Reactors Number One and Number Two continued operating until April 27 even though contamination was being sucked in through the ventilation system. Reactor Number Three had been shut down, but workers were still inside the building to supervise the cooling process. While the reactors could have been kept operating to supply electricity for the emergency work, it is not clear why standby generators were not used instead.

of the disaster and its possible consequences was reported to the government leaders. That same day, the decision was made to evacuate Pripyat. Eventually, 170 towns would be evacuated in all.

Fighting the Reactor Fire

Firefighters had continued to flood the reactor area with water, but this was causing too much radioactive steam to be released into the air. It was also having little effect on the smoldering graphite. It was vital to start plugging the crater. Scientists suggested dropping heavy, heat-resistant materials from the air into the reactor crater. At first, helicopters flew above the destroyed reactor and dropped sacks of sand, repeating the action over and over again, but the method was too slow. At the rate the helicopters were dropping sand, it would take weeks to put the fire out. It was also necessary to keep opening hatches and doors in order to allow officers to drop the sandbags, exposing them and the pilots to great risk.

Soon the helicopters were modified to carry huge nets outside their cabins, which could be released with the push of a button, so that larger amounts of material could be dropped at less risk. Scientists also modified the sand itself. Instead of dropping pure sand, they began to mix it with boron to help absorb neutrons. Lead and dolomite were also dropped to help cool the core and clay to help block up the crater. It would, by estimate, require almost 4,000 short tons (3,629 t) of this sand mixture to extinguish the reactor fire, which would take at least 40 helicopter trips.

Fortunate Mistakes

While the actions taken to put out the core fire at Chernobyl ultimately worked, it was really only luck. Many contradictory measures were taken, and no one could predict what might happen as a result. Using large amounts of water to attempt to put out the graphite fire was a mistake, as it released radioactive steam and increased the weight of water pressing down on the reactor's foundation. Competent nuclear physicists should have been sent to Chernobyl immediately, instead of 18 hours after the explosion; they could have prevented the use of so much water.

The decision to cover the reactor with sand and clay was also a mistake, as it decreased the ability of the reactor fire to release its heat. If liquid nitrogen had been used sooner, then the partial meltdown that happened would not have taken place. The Soviet government claimed that the positive outcome was a result of scientific strategy. But in reality, it was a lucky accident after a series of mistakes. Experts also feel that if the Soviet scientists had been able to contact their colleagues around the world and draw upon their experience, the correct solutions might have been applied sooner.

However, once the reactor was capped with its fill of sand and clay, the situation inside the reactor actually grew worse. The sand still allowed gases to escape from the reactor. Even without a steady supply of oxygen, the fissile materials inside the reactor continued to create high temperatures. As the reactor's red-hot core, with an estimated temperature of more than 4,500 degrees Fahrenheit (2,482° C), continued to burn, scientists began to fear that an actual meltdown would occur if the core were to burn through its concrete base into a pool of water located beneath the reactor vault. This could cause an even stronger explosion that would spread all the uranium, plutonium, and other radioactive products over a much wider area.

Something had to be done to stop the reactor from burning. And, the Soviet government would not be able to suppress news of the disaster for much longer. A radioactive cloud was drifting toward Europe. It was only a matter of time before someone noticed it. ⌐

*People all over Europe would soon be looking to Chernobyl
and what had happened there.*

*Because of the lack of information available,
many reports made exaggerated claims about the accident.*

THE WORLD FINDS OUT

E ven though the events of April 26
constituted the worst nuclear accident
in history, the rest of the world knew nothing
about Chernobyl in the first several days after the
explosion. The Soviet government did not yet

realize the full scope of the accident, and once they did, they followed established procedures and kept information about the accident from both the Soviet people and the rest of the world. But it would not be long before the telltale signs of a nuclear accident crept out of Chernobyl.

TESTING THE AIR

All nuclear power plants around the world routinely monitor and test the air and their own personnel as precautions to make sure their plant and safety systems are working. On April 28, workers at the Forsmark Nuclear Power Plant, north of Stockholm, Sweden, began receiving warning signals from their air monitors, indicating that there was an unusually high level of radiation in the air. At first, Swedish officials feared that the radiation was being produced by one of their own plants, but after running safety checks and inspections, they realized the levels were not coming from their plants. Workers arriving at the plant were setting off monitors, and when their clothing was tested with a Geiger counter (a device that measures radiation), it exceeded normal contamination levels. Tests on the dirt and vegetation outside the plant tested high for contamination as well. Whatever the source of radiation, it was not local to the power plant, and it indicated that somewhere in the world a major nuclear event had taken place. But where?

The winds were coming from the direction of the Soviet Union, and that is where officials first looked for news of a nuclear accident. Swedish officials questioned the Soviet government, which denied having any explanation for the unusually high readings. But the cloud of radioactivity that had been created by the Chernobyl explosion was on the move. Meteorologists traced the wind patterns and found that air currents were blowing across the Ukraine, into the Baltic States, and then leaving the Soviet Union to circle Poland, Czechoslovakia, and Germany, then into the Netherlands. These winds were blowing radioactive particles over other countries, whose governments demanded to know what had taken place.

The First Announcement

Finally, after demands for an explanation from Sweden, the Soviet government made an announcement on April 28, saying:

[A]n accident has occurred at the Chernobyl nuclear power plant as one of the reactors was damaged. Measures are being taken to eliminate the consequences of the accident. Aid is being given to those affected. A government commission has been set up.[1]

While the government refused to provide any more detailed information, individuals were able to provide more insight into what might have actually taken place. An amateur radio operator in the Netherlands reported receiving a radio transmission from a radio operator near Chernobyl. The operator claimed that the reactor was burning and that hundreds of people were dead or wounded. With very little information to go by, many foreign media groups picked up this dramatic, but unconfirmed, story. Part of the story was quoted in a *Time* magazine article:

Home Remedies

People who discovered that they had been—or could be—exposed to radiation often tried folk remedies to counteract the effects. These included actions such as eating cucumbers or drinking fresh milk or mineral water to supposedly counteract the effects of radiation. Those in the Soviet Union in particular believed that drinking vodka, an alcoholic beverage, could also help. Nurses in the Pripyat hospital even gave vodka to each of the firefighters who were the first to reach Chernobyl after the explosion. Unfortunately, it only made them sicker.

The [radio operator from Chernobyl] cried, "We heard heavy explosions! You can't imagine what's happening here with all the deaths and fire. I'm here 20 miles from it, and in fact I don't know what to do. I don't know if our leaders know what to do because this is a real disaster. Please tell the world to help us."[2]

Even with increased pressure from governments around the world—especially those whose countries were in the path of the radioactive fallout—the Soviet Union hesitated to release any more information or even ask for help, because that would mean revealing the true extent of the accident.

Asking for Help

Soon, however, the Soviets realized that they were going to need the assistance and expertise of those outside their country. The first indication was on Tuesday morning, April 29, when a science specialist from the Soviet embassy appeared, unannounced and without an appointment, at the office of the agency that represented West Germany's nuclear power industry. He asked whether the Germans knew anyone who could advise the Soviet Union on how to extinguish a graphite fire. Moscow invited a noted US expert in bone marrow transplants, Dr. Robert Gale, to come to Chernobyl and aid the victims there. This action alerted many experts in the nuclear industry, since bone marrow procedures were used in cases where patients had had severe radiation exposure.

PROTECTING PEOPLE

The continuing lack of information angered people around the world, especially those whom the radiation affected. In Europe, many measures were put into effect

Glasnost

When the Chernobyl accident occurred, leader Mikhail Gorbachev had only been in power as the general secretary of the Communist Party of the Soviet Union for a little over a year. Gorbachev represented people in the Soviet Union who were tired of the Communist system and the corruption and economic failure it had created there. Gorbachev adopted a new policy, known as *glasnost*, which is the Russian word for "openness." Gorbachev seemed eager to form more open relationships with other countries, as well as wanting to change the way the Soviet Union was governed. However, the established Communist leaders did not want glasnost and were not willing to give up their old ways.

When Chernobyl occurred, Gorbachev was caught between the established secrecy of the older Communist leaders and the desire to be open and honest in its international relations. For several days following the accident, the old government policy of secrecy prevented news of the incident from being released, until Gorbachev realized that they would not get the help they needed unless they told the world what had happened. Gorbachev realized that hiding the incident went against his policy of glasnost, after which the first public announcement was made on Soviet television. However, he would be criticized for his delay in admitting to the world what had taken place.

to protect people, such as banning the sale of fresh milk (which can be contaminated if cows eat contaminated grass), ordering owners of outdoor produce stands to wash and cover their produce, and telling people to avoid drinking rainwater. In Poland, children were given iodine solutions to help keep their bodies from absorbing radioactive elements. The US government issued travel warnings, urging people, especially women and children, not to travel to Poland. European citizens were frightened and angry about the lack of information from the Soviets. As one resident of Warsaw, Poland, later said:

> We can understand an accident, it could happen to anyone, but that the Soviets said nothing and let our children suffer exposure to this cloud [of radiation] for days is unforgivable.[3]

Panic in Kiev

On May 6, Anatoli Romanenko, the health minister for the Ukraine, went on television and urged the people of Kiev to wash their vegetables, close their windows, and stay inside. Rumors were flying, and soon people were flocking to train stations to buy tickets out of the area. Gasoline quickly ran out. Although the radiation soon blew away from Kiev, and officials assured people that the air quality was now within safe limits, most people refused to believe them. The government's previous failure to tell the truth about what had actually happened made people distrustful and brought the city to panic levels.

Wrapping It Up

In the meantime, something had to be done about the reactor that was still smoldering, after helicopters dropped bags of sand and other materials into the core from April 27 to May 3. On May 8, large amounts of liquid nitrogen were brought to the area and injected into every possible space surrounding the reactor. This cloud of cold nitrogen finally worked to start bringing the reactor temperature down on May 10. By May 11, a Moscow television station announced that the danger of the reactor burning had passed. However, people around the world still had yet to hear the full details of the disaster.

Coming Clean

Finally, on May 14, 1986, Soviet leader Mikhail Gorbachev appeared on Soviet television to give a speech that would be broadcast all over the world. He finally described the Chernobyl accident, which, only a week earlier, Soviet officials had described as only a "minor event." Gorbachev said:

> *All of you know that we have been struck by a misfortune recently—the accident at the Chernobyl nuclear power plant.*

It has painfully affected the Soviet people and troubled the international community. We have, for the first time, confronted in reality the dreadful force of nuclear energy that got out of control. [4]

Chernobyl was no longer a secret. Now it was time to start cleaning up, and to face the consequences.

Firefighters decontaminate a radioactive truck
arriving from eastern Europe.

Farmers in Germany were instructed by the government to plow over their crops of leafy green vegetables due to radioactive contamination.

THE AFTERMATH

The Chernobyl disaster had caused death, destruction, and economic hardships, both in the area around the plant and reaching farther into Europe. Eastern Europe would suffer a yearlong ban on any agricultural products coming from its fields, where contamination was heaviest. But the Soviets had other worries. They still needed to find a way to contain any further leaking of radioactive material. The graphite fire in the reactor core had finally been extinguished on May 11, but radioactive particles were still escaping from the core.

The Cleanup

Soviet scientists decided that the best way to contain the core and stop the spread of radiation would be to cover the remains of the reactor in a thick shell of steel and concrete. This shell, which was nicknamed "the coffin" or "the sarcophagus," would require 12 million cubic feet (339,802 cu m) of concrete and 3,000 short tons (2,721 t) of steel to construct. Finished, it would stand 28 stories high, almost as high as the original reactor building. And it would need to be strong. As Medvedev comments in his book *The Legacy of Chernobyl*:

Smart Shoppers

In the aftermath of the Chernobyl accident, one of the primary concerns was that people might consume food that had soaked up radiation. Locals tried to avoid eating foods known to soak up a lot of radiation, such as mushrooms and milk. Shoppers made sure to ask food vendors where their produce had come from. In Kiev, regulations were put in place at markets that all food had to be tested and certified as non-contaminated before it could be sold.

Europeans, too, were concerned about consuming contaminated produce grown in eastern Europe. Many French shoppers used Geiger counters to inspect the produce in markets before purchasing it.

The giant sarcophagus, which surrounds the destroyed reactor core containing nearly 1,000 kg [more than 2,200 pounds] of plutonium must remain intact for far longer even than the Egyptian pyramids.[1]

But who would build the sarcophagus, especially in the highly radioactive conditions that existed around the destroyed reactor? As soon as this plan to build the cover was announced, Soviet officials were already insisting that it had to be constructed within just a few months so that the other reactors in the plant could be put back online. They did not realize that before work could even begin, it would be necessary to clean up the chunks of graphite and conduct decontamination before anyone could even enter the area. At first, this cleanup was attempted using remote-controlled bulldozers and robots, but these did not work well, and robots did not last long in the high radioactivity.

In May, officials realized that they would need a huge number of people to enter the site for cleanup and construction. They sent out a call across the entire Soviet Union for 400,000 workers to participate. Many young men who were carrying out mandatory military service were required to help with the cleanup. Reserve soldiers and officers were also obligated to participate. Since the areas surrounding the destroyed reactor were so high in radiation, these workers, who were called "liquidators," would be allowed to work inside the contamination for only 90 seconds at a time. If anyone remained in the area for more than 30 minutes, their entire nervous system would be destroyed. Many of them knew nothing about the dangers of radioactivity. Others had had some chemical military training. There was a shortage of proper protective equipment, and

A Liquidator's View

In the summer of 1986, a young man named Sergei worked as a liquidator at Chernobyl. He later moved to the United States and was interviewed by Mark Resnicoff about his experiences. Sergei was only 30, a chemist in the Soviet military. When asked whether the liquidators were kept in the work zone for too long a period of time, he said:

Yes, it happened in my case and in many other cases—countless, actually—for several reasons. One was that there was not enough of individual dosimeters available during spring-summer of 1986 for everybody; only "civics," engineers and scientists, had them. We "military," army reservists, did not. Shortage was a common word. Another reason was that [there were] not enough [subs] available, particularly of mid-rank officers, so doses accumulated by many of us during July-August-September of 1986 were artificially lowered in the paperwork.[2]

Sergei has survived his own radiation exposure at Chernobyl, although he has continued to suffer health issues.

Liquidators, lacking protective gear,
made their own suits from lead sheets.

not enough dosimeters to track the radiation dose of every worker. But despite the dangers, the promise of high pay and extra benefits was enough to make some people sign up.

The liquidators had many jobs in addition to constructing the sarcophagus. They built concrete pits and buried all moveable objects in the vicinity of the plant that had become contaminated, such as vehicles, trees, and even topsoil. Decontamination chemicals were sprayed on the roofs and streets of Pripyat, since, at that time, it was still hoped that residents would be able to return. With so much to do, cleanup efforts quickly fell behind schedule, and the Soviet government ordered that two of the other Chernobyl reactors be restarted before the sarcophagus was even complete.

The sarcophagus itself was built using concrete blocks that were prefabricated at a distance from the reactor, but the roads to the plant were not wide enough to allow the necessary construction vehicles to transport them easily. A crane had to be used to lift the sections of concrete block into place. It would be December 1986—two months behind schedule—before the sarcophagus was completed.

Even as the liquidators were building the sarcophagus and cleaning up the area, those workers and firefighters who had been the first to respond to the accident were dying. Some had died immediately afterward because of high exposure to radiation and burns, but others took longer to show the signs of severe radiation poisoning. Many of the first responders had received doses of radiation that were much higher than normal.

Most of the 70 firefighters and plant workers who were on duty the night of the explosion died within ten years. Soon the liquidators were also becoming ill, since many of them were inadequately protected and had received much higher doses than the official records actually showed. Of those who participated in the cleanup, 4,000 died within 15 years, and another 70,000 were permanently disabled.

Who Is to Blame?

Both Dyatlov and Bryukhanov had also received high doses of radiation, but doctors felt they would survive for at least five years. In addition to their health problems, they found themselves being blamed for the accident. In 1987, they were put on trial, along with four other managers from the Chernobyl plant. Despite the fact that it was partly due to pressure from the Soviet government

that the accident occurred at all, and that much of
the secrecy immediately after the accident was due
to government attempts to keep news of the accident
from reaching the world, these four men were
charged with incompetency in running the plant,
and negligence in how they handled the aftermath
of the explosion. The Soviet government needed
to show that it was human error and not the design
of the nuclear plants themselves that was at fault.
Otherwise, it might be forced to shut down similar
RBMK reactors and to put off building new ones.
An article in *Time* magazine described the trial:

> When asked whether they understood the case against them,
> the men admitted some guilt but denied outright responsibility
> for the accident. . . . [Bryukhanov] conceded that he had
> been partially negligent. He insisted, however, that he was
> not guilty of safety violations. Dyatlov provided the most
> emotional moment. Grabbing a microphone and holding it
> close, he denied in a firm voice that he was directly to blame
> for the death of any plant workers. Then Dyatlov added,
> "With so many human deaths, I cannot say I am completely
> innocent."[3]

Dyatlov and Bryukhanov were convicted and
sentenced to ten years in prison, although they

each served just five years. In 1995, Dyatlov died of cancer shortly after his release. Bryukhanov is reportedly still living.

The reactor had been encased in concrete and the contamination had been minimized as much as possible. Blame had been assigned and the Soviet newspaper *Pravda* declared that the accident occurred as a result of rule violations by the plant's operators, not because of the plant's design. The immediate results of the accident had been dealt with but Chernobyl would have a much longer-lasting impact.

Workers at the Plant

Of the workers who had been in the plant at the time of the accident, Toptunov died by May 12, when the tissue in his lungs rotted from beta burns, suffocating him. Akimov had a bone marrow transplant, but the skin on one of his legs turned black and slipped off, exposing bone, and his intestines disintegrated. Only Yuvchenko survived, burned and requiring many skin grafts, but without internal damage.

*Bryukhanov, left, and others were tried for their roles
in the Chernobyl disaster.*

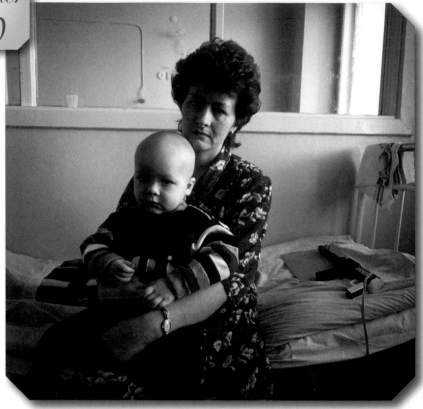

Children developed leukemia and other forms of cancer as a result of radiation exposure.

THE LEGACY

Decades after the Chernobyl accident took place, the effects of the disaster still impacted many people, particularly when it comes to health. The biggest change that took place in the years after the Chernobyl accident was the fall of the Soviet Union. The system of Communist government was already weakened at the time of the accident. Some experts believe that the failure of the government to tell the truth about the incident and its impact on its citizens helped to bring about the fall of the Communist regime. In August 1991, the Soviet Union officially ceased to exist as a nation, breaking up into 15 separate independent nations.

Official numbers for how many people died as a result of Chernobyl, both immediately and from long-term health issues, have never been given. However, in April 1992 the Ukraine minister for Chernobyl estimated that as many as 8,000 people in his country alone had died. Many of them lived in areas that received high levels of radioactive fallout and suffered from radiation-related health issues such as cardiovascular disease and cancer. Children have suffered from thyroid cancer and leukemia. According to the Nuclear Regulatory Commission:

Chernobyl Syndrome

There is actually a name for the psychological ailment that many people suffer as a result of their experiences after the Chernobyl accident. Called the "Chernobyl syndrome," its sufferers feel helpless and overwhelmed about the possible consequences to their health, especially since the health impact of the disaster may not even be seen in some people until 2016 at the earliest. They also feel like they are victims of circumstances they cannot control and have little confidence in their ability to help themselves. The syndrome has led to an increase in alcohol abuse and clinical depression for millions of people.

[A] large number of children and adolescents . . . received substantial radiation doses in the thyroid after drinking milk contaminated with radioactive iodine. To date, about 4,000 thyroid cancer cases have been detected among these children. Although 99 percent of these children were successfully treated, nine children and adolescents in [Ukraine, Belarus, and Russia] died from thyroid cancer.[1]

THE ENVIRONMENTAL TOLL

While the effects of contamination can be seen in human health trends, the accident also had a lasting effect on the environment. In addition to entire villages and cities being abandoned, many formerly rich agricultural areas have also been abandoned, either because of radiation levels or because of contamination of the soil that makes it unsafe to grow food there. Many native plant and animal species have died out or mutated. Farm animals, such as pigs and cows, were born with mutations such as cleft lips and extra limbs. In 1992, a reporter from the *Moscow News,* Vladimir Kolinko, visited a farm not far from the Chernobyl plant:

At the animal farm . . . I was shown a suckling pig whose head looked like that of a frog: instead of eyes there were large

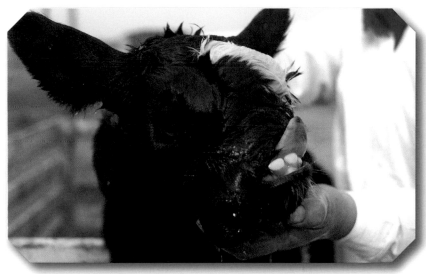

*Malformations in animals became common
after the radioactive fallout from Chernobyl.*

*tissue outgrowths with a cornea or pupil. "One of the many
freaks of nature," [the farm veterinary surgeon said.] . . .
"They usually die soon after birth, but this one has survived."
The farm is small: 350 cows and 87 pigs. During the first
year after the accident the birth of 64 freaks was registered at
the farm. . . . Most often calves are born without a head or
limbs, without eyes or ribs. The pigs are distinguished by . . .
deformation of the skull and so on.*[2]

As of 2010, the three independent nations
that were most heavily affected by radiation
contamination from Chernobyl—Belarus, Russia,

and Ukraine—were still struggling with the economic legacy of the accident. They struggled to provide care for those whose health has been affected, while trying to establish healthy economies as new countries.

Despite the negative effects on the environment, the Chernobyl disaster and the consequent abandonment of many villages also allowed some animal species to thrive. The abandoned area has become somewhat of a wildlife sanctuary. For example, Przewalski's horses, a rare breed of horse that had been bred only in captivity for several decades, were released into the area after scientists noticed that other hoofed animals were doing well in the radioactive area.

Chernobyl Today

The two remaining operating reactors at the Chernobyl plant were shut down in 2000. As of 2010, areas around the Chernobyl plant were divided into zones of contamination, based on how much radiation affected them and whether they are safe for human habitation. The area directly surrounding the plant was a closed zone, with controlled zones extending in concentric rings from the plant, depending on the amount of radiation still found there. These zones are controlled by the government and monitored for human activity and levels of contamination. Some elderly people have returned to live in exclusion zones but their food must be transported in and they have regular medical checkups. The government tried to protect tourists and other people from the heaviest contamination areas. However, because some of the places where contaminated materials were buried during the cleanup are known only to the former liquidators, not every "hot spot" has been mapped.

Nuclear Tourism

Amazingly enough, as radiation levels around Chernobyl have fallen to safer levels, it has become a popular tourist destination. People come from all over the world to see the area, as short visits do not pose a health risk. They must be accompanied by an official government guide, carry a Geiger counter, and stay away from clearly marked areas of higher radiation. One such tourist, Charles Hawley, made an excursion to the exclusion zone in 2006 and wrote an article about his experiences there:

The fruit orchards are heavy with unpicked, radioactive fruit that is left rotting on the branches. . . . Vegetation is taking over the streets. The city of Pripyat—once a bustling Soviet city—is now an image of absolute decay, its wide boulevards empty but for the winds and the occasional wild boar or feral dog. At one end of its once ostentatious main street, the city's cultural center still stands, debris spilling out of its front doors and down the stairs. . . . [B]ehind the cultural center, an amusement park—Ferris wheel rusted, bumper cars overturned—is still waiting for children who will never come.[3]

Some of the materials were buried in clay-lined pits near the plant. But some of those pits have started leaking contaminated materials into the soil. The bottom soil of the Dnieper and Pripyat Rivers has been found to contain high levels of radioactive materials, contaminating the water supply of many people in the area. One of the biggest concerns is the state of the sarcophagus around the destroyed reactor. It was built quickly, and cracks have developed in the structure. Its condition is uncertain, especially since it occupies a high-radiation environment, which can quickly degrade building materials.

In 1997, the European community and Ukraine agreed to establish a fund to help Ukraine take the existing sarcophagus and transform it into a stable and more environmentally safe system. It also provided workers and equipment to make emergency repairs to the roof beams of the sarcophagus. This plan, called the Chernobyl Shelter Implementation Plan, was created to construct a new safe shelter at a cost of more than $700 million. The design includes an arch-shaped steel structure, which can be slid across the existing sarcophagus on rails and should remain functional for 100 years. In September

2007, Ukraine contracted with a French company
for construction of the shelter, but work, which was
originally scheduled for completion in 2012, had
not yet begun as of 2010. According to the Web site
Powertechnology.com:

> On 7 January 2010, the Ukrainian Government passed
> a state law to transform the Chernobyl shelter facility into
> an environmentally safe system in order to protect the
> surroundings from radiation. The [program] will be executed
> in four stages. In the first stage, nuclear fuel will be moved to
> a storage facility, which will be completed by 2013. In the
> second stage which will be completed by 2025, all the reactors
> will be deactivated. The third stage involves maintaining the
> reactors until radiation drops to an acceptable level and is
> envisaged to be completed by 2045. The fourth and the final
> stage involves dismantling the reactors and clearing the site,
> which is expected to be completed by 2065.[4]

Despite the Chernobyl accident and the lessons
learned about RBMK reactors, there are still 15 of
these nuclear plants operating in Russia, Ukraine,
and Lithuania. Although improvements have been
made in their design, there are still concerns about
them, particularly those that were built before
Chernobyl. In 1996, the International Atomic

Young Deaths

Some of the most poignant accounts of Chernobyl came from children who were there at the time of the accident. One former citizen recalled, "In the seventh grade I found out about death . . . Yulia, Katya, Vadim, Oksana, Oleg, and . . . Andrei. 'We'll die, and then we'll become science,' Andrei used to say. 'We'll die and everyone will forget us,' Katya said. 'When I die, don't bury me at the cemetery, I'm afraid of the cemetery, there are only dead people and crows there,' said Oksana. 'Bury me in the field.' Yulia used to just cry. The whole sky is alive for me now when I look at it because they're all there."[5]

Energy Commission established the Nuclear Safety Convention to agree on international standards for nuclear safety and monitor compliance. As of April 2009, there were 436 nuclear power plants operating in 30 countries.

Chernobyl will forever be a testament to the dangers of nuclear energy when improperly handled. Many people hope the lessons learned about safety procedures and precautions and the importance of open communication will never be forgotten. As the world seeks new sources of energy and takes a fresh look at nuclear power, the lessons of Chernobyl are more important than ever.

A memorial to Chernobyl's victims stands outside the ruins of Reactor Number Four.

TIMELINE

1977	1984	1986
The V. I. Lenin Nuclear Power Station is opened near Chernobyl, Ukraine.	Reactor Number Four of the Chernobyl nuclear plant is brought online in March.	Preparations are made for conducting a turbine test on Reactor Number Four on April 25.

1986	1986	1986
At 1:24 a.m., the reactor overheats and causes a steam explosion. A second explosion ejects graphite chunks and reactor fuel.	At 1:28 a.m., the first firefighters arrive from Pripyat.	On April 27, helicopters begin dropping sand on the reactor fire. Official evacuation of Pripyat begins in the afternoon.

1986

On April 26, operators begin reducing power in the reactor at 12:28 a.m.

1986

The test begins at 1:23:04 a.m., and temperatures increase rapidly in the reactor.

1986

At 1:23:40 a.m., the operator initiates an emergency shutdown and inserts all the control rods into the reactor. This causes a power spike.

1986

On April 28, radiation is detected by the Forsmark Nuclear Power Plant in Sweden.

1986

On April 28, Soviet officials finally announce that an accident has taken place.

1986

An 18-mile (20-km) zone around the Chernobyl plant is designated for evacuation on May 2.

TIMELINE

1986	1986	1986
On May 8, liquid nitrogen is injected into the foundations of Reactor Building Number Four.	The first firefighter dies from radiation sickness on May 9.	The fire in Reactor Number Four is finally extinguished on May 11.

1987	1991	1997
In July, six plant operators, including Bryukhanov, go on trial for negligence and are found guilty.	The Soviet Union dissolves.	A fund is started to pay for the construction of a new protective shelter on the Reactor Number Four sarcophagus.

1986

On May 14, Soviet leader Mikhail Gorbachev admits that a serious accident has taken place at Chernobyl.

1986

Starting in May, liquidators are brought to Chernobyl to begin the cleanup operation.

1986

The sarcophagus around the destroyed reactor is completed in December.

2000

The last operating reactor at the Chernobyl plant is shut down, and the plant is decommissioned.

2002

The exclusion zone around the Chernobyl plant is opened to tourists.

Essential Facts

Date of Event

April 26, 1986

Place of Event

Chernobyl Nuclear Power Plant, Pripyat, Ukraine, USSR

Key Players

❖ Aleksandr Akimov

❖ Viktor Bryukhanov, plant director

❖ Anatoly Dyatlov

❖ Leonid Toptunov

❖ Sasha Yuvchenko

HIGHLIGHTS OF EVENT

❖ Explosions occurred at the Chernobyl nuclear power plant
   on April 26, 1986, releasing radioactive material into the
   atmosphere and destroying the reactor building. Two men were
   killed immediately in the explosion. Hundreds of others died in
   the following weeks from acute radiation poisoning. Thousands
   more died as a result of health problems brought on by radiation
   exposure.

❖ The surrounding areas of the Chernobyl power plant were
   evacuated beginning on April 27, but radiation drifted into
   other parts of Europe and caused contamination.

❖ The reactor fire burned uncontrollably for several days but was
   finally extinguished on May 11. The reactor was encased in a steel
   and concrete sarcophagus, completed in December 1986.

❖ The Soviet Union was widely criticized for withholding news of
   the accident from the rest of the world.

QUOTE

"It seemed as if the world was coming to an end...I could not
believe my eyes. I saw the reactor ruined by the explosion. I was the
first man in the world to see this. As a nuclear engineer, I realized
all the consequences of what had happened. It was a nuclear hell."
—Anatoly Dyatlov, *who was in the control room when the accident occurred.*

GLOSSARY

atom
> The smallest part of an element that still retains the characteristics of that element.

control rods
> Devices used to control nuclear fission by regulating the fission process.

core
> The part of a nuclear reactor that contains nuclear fuel.

dosimeter
> A device used to measure a person's radiation exposure.

fallout
> Microscopic particles of radioactive materials in the atmosphere following a nuclear explosion.

fission
> The process of splitting the nucleus of one atom and releasing energy.

glasnost
> The Russian word for "openness," and a government policy in 1980s USSR.

meltdown
> When a nuclear reactor overheats, melting its fuel rods and causing the release of radioactive materials and radiation.

mutation
> A change in cell structure that can be caused by radiation exposure, often creating deformities in plants and animals.

neutron
> A particle with no electrical charge, found in the nucleus of an atom, that binds protons together.

nuclear
> A type of energy that comes from particles found in atoms.

nuclear reactor
> A piece of equipment where a nuclear reaction can be started, maintained, and controlled, generating energy.

plutonium
> A natural radioactive element found in uranium and used in nuclear weapons.

radioactivity
> Radiation emitted by a nuclear reaction.

rem
> Roentgen equivalent man; a measure of the effects of different radioactive waves on humans.

roentgen
> The original unit used to measure radiation exposure in humans.

turbine
> A machine with blades driven by steam, which produces electrical energy.

uranium
> An element extracted from certain minerals and used as nuclear fuel.

ADDITIONAL RESOURCES

SELECTED BIBLIOGRAPHY

Atkins, Stephen E. *Historical Encyclopedia of Atomic Energy*. Westport, CT: Greenwood, 2000. Print.

"Chernobyl Accident." *World-nuclear.org*. World Nuclear Association, Aug. 2010. Web. 5 Sept. 2010.

Medvedev, Zhores. *The Legacy of Chernobyl*. New York: Norton, 1992. Print.

United States Nuclear Regulatory Commission. "Backgrounder on Chernobyl Nuclear Power Plant Accident." *NRC.gov*. Nuclear Regulatory Commission, 30 Apr. 2009. Web. 5 Sept. 2010.

FURTHER READINGS

Ingram, W. Scott. *Environmental Disasters: The Chernobyl Nuclear Disaster*. New York: Facts on File, 2005. Print.

Lusted, Marcia Amidon, and Greg Lusted. *Building History: A Nuclear Power Plant*. Farmington Hills, MI: Lucent, 2005. Print.

Nelson, David Eric. *Perspectives on Modern World History: Chernobyl*. Farmington Hills, MI: Greenhaven, 2010. Print.

Parker, Vic. *When Disaster Struck: Chernobyl 1986*. Chicago: Raintree, 2006. Print.

Walker, Linda. *Children in Crisis: Living After Chernobyl — Ira's Story*. Milwaukee, WI: World Almanac Library, 2005. Print.

Web Links

To learn more about the Chernobyl disaster, visit ABDO Publishing Company online at **www.abdopublishing.com**. Web sites about the Chernobyl disaster are featured on our Book Links page. These links are routinely monitored and updated to provide the most current information available.

Places to Visit

Atomic Testing Museum
755 E. Flamingo Road, Las Vegas, NV 89119
702-794-5161
http://www.atomictestingmuseum.org
This museum has many exhibits on nuclear power and nuclear weaponry.

National Museum of Nuclear Science and History
601 Eubank Blvd SE, Albuquerque, NM 87123
505-245-2137
http://www.nuclearmuseum.org
This museum hosts permanent and changing exhibits related to nuclear science.

SOURCE NOTES

Chapter 1. 1:23 a.m., April 26, 1986

1. W. Scott Ingram. *The Chernobyl Nuclear Disaster*. New York: Facts on File, 2005. Print. 82.

2. David Erik Nelson. *Perspectives on Modern World History: Chernobyl*. Farmington Hills, MI: Greenhaven, 2010. Print. 156.

Chapter 2. In the Beginning

1. Zhores Medvedev. *The Legacy of Chernobyl*. New York: Norton, 1992. Print. 14.

Chapter 3. Chernobyl's Reactors

None.

Chapter 4. It Was Just a Test . . .

1. David Erik Nelson. *Perspectives on Modern World History: Chernobyl*. Farmington Hills, MI: Greenhaven, 2010. Print. 47.

2. Ibid.

3. "Chernobyl Concepts." *Hyperphysic*. Georgia State University, n.d. Web. 15 Aug. 2010.

4. Zhores Medvedev. *The Legacy of Chernobyl*. New York: Norton, 1992. Print. 24-25.

5. Ibid. 37.

Chapter 5. Fires, Confusion, and Chaos

1. Vivienne Parry. "How I Survived Chernobyl." *guardian.co.uk*. The Guardian News and Media Limited, 24 Aug. 2004. Web. 22 Sept. 2010.

2. Zhores Medvedev. *The Legacy of Chernobyl*. New York: Norton, 1992. Print. 52.

Chapter 6. The First Effects
1. Zhores Medvedev. *The Legacy of Chernobyl*. New York: Norton, 1992. Print. 133.
2. Ibid. 142.

Chapter 7. Government Response
1. Zhores Medvedev. *The Legacy of Chernobyl*. New York: Norton, 1992. Print. 50.
2. Ibid. 52.

Chapter 8. The World Finds Out
1. Serge Schemann. "Power Reactor Damaged." *The New York Times on the Web*. New York Times Company, 28 Apr. 1986. Web. 24 Sept. 2010.
2. John Greenwald. "Deadly Meltdown." *Time Magazine*. Time, 12 May 1986. Web. 24 Sept. 2010.
3. Ibid.
4. Gulnoza Saidazimova and Claire Bigg. "Chornobyl 20 Years After: Liquidators Recall Disaster, Speak Of Life After." *Radio Free Europe Radio Liberty*. Radio Free Europe/Radio Liberty, 20 Apr. 2006. Web. 24 Sept. 2010.

Chapter 9. The Aftermath
1. Zhores Medvedev. *The Legacy of Chernobyl*. New York: Norton, 1992. Print. 20.
2. Mark Resnicoff. "Interview with Sergei B." *Chernobyl and Eastern Europe*. Mark Resnicoff, 2010. Web. 4 Sept. 2010.
3. John Greenwald and Ken Olsen. "Disaster Judgment at Chernobyl." *Time*. Time, 20 July 1987. Web. 24 Sept. 2010.

Source Notes Continued

Chapter 10. The Legacy

1. United States Nuclear Regulatory Commission. "Background on Chernobyl Nuclear Power Plant Accident." *U.S.NRC.* United States Nuclear Regulatory Commission, Apr. 2009. Web. 24 Sept. 2010.

2. Zhores Medvedev. *The Legacy of Chernobyl.* New York: Norton, 1992. Print. 142. 116.

3. Charles Hawley. "A Visit to the Exclusion Zone." *Spiegel Online International.* Spiegel Online International, 18 Apr. 2006. Web. 24 Sept. 2010.

4. "Chernobyl Nuclear Power Plant Decommissioning, Ukraine." *Power-technology.com.* Net Resources International, 2010. Web. 5 Sept. 2010.

5. David Erik Nelson. *Perspectives on Modern World History: Chernobyl.* Farmington Hills, MI: Greenhaven, 2010. Print. 183.

INDEX

Index Continued

ABOUT THE AUTHOR

Marcia Amidon Lusted is the author of more than 40 books and many magazine articles for young readers. She is also an assistant editor for Cobblestone Publishing. She lives in New Hampshire.

PHOTO CREDITS